Linux

A complete guide to Linux command line for beginners, and how to get started with the Linux operating system!

Table of Contents

Introduction

Thank you for taking the time to pick up this book about Linux.

Linux is an operating system that is seriously underrated, and in the eyes of many is far superior to any Windows or Mac OS available. Using Linux as your operating system can allow you to better improve the performance of your computer, save yourself money on licensing and applications, and even protect you from malicious viruses.

This book covers the basics of Linux, explaining the different versions that are available, along with their varying capabilities. In the following chapters you will discover how the Linux OS functions, how to install it on your computer, and even how to begin using the command line to perform various tasks.

Whether you want to use Linux for all of your computing needs, or if you're simply curious about this revolutionary open-source operating system, this book provides a solid foundation of knowledge to get you started!

Once again, thanks for choosing this book, I hope you find it to be helpful, and enjoy using Linux!

Chapter 1: What Is Linux?

Despite being one of the most widely used operating systems, those who are unfamiliar with computer technology and operating systems may not realize what Linux is or just how important it can be. Linux was created in the mid-1990s, when Windows began to dominate the market for operating systems installed on personal computers. For that reason, most people with a computer today are only familiar with Microsoft Windows. They may also be familiar with the more recent Apple operating systems, used in iPhones and MacBooks, but Linux tends to be overlooked by those not specifically interested in operating systems.

The fact is that Linux can be found anywhere from your smartphone to your vehicle, from the supercomputers in large institutions to everyday home appliances such as your refrigerator. Linux is strongly centered around the internet and technology-heavy supercomputers which help perform the calculations necessary for many of the scientific breakthroughs of our time. Linux has grown into one of the most stable and secure operating systems and is tasked with running a wealth of systems around the world, so why are many of us still out of the loop when it comes to such a powerful and prominent system?

How Does an Operating System Work?

Before we can have a full understanding of what Linux is and how it works, we first need to understand what an operating system is in general and how works. The operating system can be thought of as the middleman of communication between the software and hardware installed on your computer. You use a number of operating systems each and every day, but the one you most likely are familiar with is the system installed on your personal computer. This could be Windows XP, especially for older computers, Windows 7, Windows 8, or the most recent Windows 10. MacBook users will likely be familiar with a version of Mac OS such as Mac OS X. In any case, these operating systems are tasked with managing all the resources within your desktop or laptop.

There are many pieces to an operating system, each with its own set of functions to help your computer perform the tasks that you assign to it. For Linux, these pieces include:

The Bootloader - This is the software that enables your computer to boot up or start the programs that you need to use. This is generally a screen that will appear as your operating system starts up. The boot loader starts all the processes that are required to present your system in a useable way.

The Kernel - The kernel is a program that controls the entire operating system. It can be thought of as the core of the system and it is tasked with managing the CPU, memory, and peripheral devices. The kernel is the most basic element of an operating system, meaning that it ensures the operation of the crucial system functions.

Daemons - These are services which operate in the background. They enable processes necessary only for certain commands. For example, they manage the printing of documents, sounds, and scheduling, amongst others. These services generally start as soon as the computer is booted or the desktop starts.

The Shell - In the early days of Linux, many people felt intimidated by the Linux command line, or shell. The shell allows users to issue tasks to the computer via commands typed into a text interface. This was not particularly user-friendly and seemed a daunting task to users with little knowledge of technology or coding. As the technology improved, the user interface was developed to appeal to those who are less tech savvy, becoming a lot more simple to use.

Graphical Server - The graphical server is what you see on the screen; it allows you to issue commands through the graphical user interface. The graphical server is known as a subsystem or X server.

Desktop Environment - This is the area where users interact with the operating system (rather than the command line method of the past). One advantage of Linux is the variety of desktop environments available to users. The desktop environments available include Unity, GNOME, Cinnamon, Enlightenment, KDE, XFCE, and many more. Each of these desktop environments offers built-in applications to help users manage their files, configure their computer, use the internet, and even play games.

Applications - Applications are programs that perform a group of coordinated tasks, like a word processor or a photo editor. Some applications may be bundled with the operating system, but there are thousands more available for download. Linux offers many applications which can be searched for, downloaded, and installed from a program (similar to Apples App Store) called Ubuntu Software Centre, which is offered as a part of Ubuntu Linux.

The Advantages of Linux

If you are already accustomed to using Microsoft Windows or Mac OS, what would be the purpose of learning to use Linux, particularly when it can be quite different from the operating system you use, and therefore, confusing to learn?

There are many reasons for learning to use Linux, some of which people may not even consider. People become so complacent with their operating systems despite facing numerous viruses, malware, spyware, slowdowns, system crashes, repairs, and even fees associated with licensing. These problems can be not only incredibly frustrating, but also expensive. Aside from the cost of repairs and protection, you may also lose valuable data. These problems are usually managed by yearly clean-ups or periodically reformatting the hard drive to ensure the system is refreshed.

Why do people spend so much to manage problems instead of fixing them? If you think there is no alternative, you generally feel that you must accept the way things are. Linux is the alternative. Once you understand that Linux can offer solutions to many of the problems you face, it opens your eyes to a whole new world free from the plagues of the mainstream operating systems.

Linux is unique in the fact that it is offered free of charge to users for installation on their computers, whereas other operating systems can cost hundreds in licensing fees. Installing these operating systems, especially across a number of computers, as in the case of a business, can be quite costly. Let's take a look at the cost of setting up a Windows server: in 2012, the price of a Windows server was about $1,200 USD. This base price excludes CALs (client access licenses) and any other software for use on the server. Linux is the clear option in terms of economic advantage as it is completely free, including everything needed to get the system up and running. It can also be installed across as many computers as required, with no accumulating fees.

How is it possible that Linux is free to install? It seems too good to be true.

Linux is distributed under an open source license. This means a number of things. Firstly, users are able to run the program how they wish and for the purpose they decide. They can study how the program works and customise the program to suit their exact needs. There are no limitations on customisation since it is open for anyone to alter. Users can then distribute either unmodified or modified copies of the software to friends, family, and neighbours, encouraging the sharing and adopting of the operating system.

Linux is a community-driven platform. The open source nature of the software encourages users to change and modify the program in order to consistently improve the platform and provide more advantages for its users. Linux is the operating system that stands for freedom and flexibility, a platform "by the people, for the people."

Aside from the obvious economic advantages of setting up Linux versus mainstream operating systems, Linux rarely requires any troubleshooting or intervention should the system be affected by malware, viruses, or any other slowdowns. In fact, Linux can essentially go many years without requiring a single reboot, and then only if the kernel requires an update. System administrators can spend less time managing servers with Linux because it allows them to essentially set and forget. Of course, basic inputs like restarting, reconfiguring, and upgrading are required, but most of the elements of the server remain static. The stability and dependability of Linux is unmatched, saving users both time and money.

Linux Distributions

Earlier, the different versions of Linux created by different users based on their specific requirements were mentioned. These modified versions of Linux are known as distributions and the different distributions of Linux are obviously suited for different types of users. What will suit a beginner to the Linux platform may not be sufficient for an advanced user. A version that is a powerful tool in the hands of an advanced user may be overwhelming for a beginner who is still learning to make use of the platform.

There are many different distributions, so you should be able to find one that fits your needs. Then, you simply download a free version of it, put it on a DVD or USB drive to install it across all the systems you need, whether in the home or business. A few of the many distributions stand out as user favorites:

- Ubuntu Linux

- Linux Mint

- Arch Linux

- Deepin

- Fedora

- Debian

- openSUSE

Each of these distributions is popular for different reasons and with different groups of users. If you are particularly skilled with computers, you may opt for a distribution with some additional features, such as Debian or Fedora. For those who are more advanced and enjoy the flexibility that comes with their skill level, they might choose a distribution like Gentoo. For those who are new to Linux (and if you are reading this book, chances are that you are new to the platform), you might want to opt for one of the simpler distributions to get your feet wet, such as Linux Mint, Ubuntu, or Deepin. As you can see, there are many different distributions for all types of skill levels and one advantage of Linux is that even when you decide on a distribution, you do not have to continue with that distribution forever. Once you are comfortable with using those newbie-friendly distributions, you can move on to one with a little more flexibility to continue learning.

Your desktop will depend on the distribution you decide to use. Some users prefer a cutting-edge user interface, such as those offered by Ubuntu and Deepin. Of course, there are also users who prefer a more standard desktop environment, like the one offered by openSUSE, KDE. It is important to note that certain distributions do carry a price tag since they hold extra features and offer user support. Examples of these distributions are Red Hat Enterprise Linux and SUSE Enterprise Linux.

For those searching for a distribution to complement their server, a big decision is deciding whether they require a desktop interface or if they are comfortable simply using the command line. The Ubuntu Server, for example, does not install a Graphic User Interface or GUI. There are advantages to this, like the fact that the server will never be in danger of being overloaded by the loading of graphics. However, it requires a solid understanding of the Linux command line, which does take a little bit of practice. You do have the option to install your own GUI on top of the Ubuntu server, which is an advantage that many Linux distributions offer. To install your GUI, you would use the command line to enter "sudo apt-get install ubuntu-desktop."

For system administrators, features are often a core focus. We will explore this in a later chapter, but we can mention now that when it comes to Linux, there is always the option for more features. Depending on the distribution you select, you may have all the features you need for your server straight out of the box, such as the case for CentOS. You may decide that you want to add the features you require as you need them, in which case Debian or Ubuntu Linux may better fit your needs.

Chapter 2: Installing And Setting Up Linux

There a couple of ways to install Linux from your current operating system. You can choose to download Linux from either a live CD or a USB drive, and then boot Linux from your system in order to install it. For beginners, this can get a little confusing, but it doesn't actually require a lot of technical knowhow and once you get through the first time, installing another system is simple if you choose to do so. For this book, we will use the example of installing Linux on a computer currently running Windows.

Installing from a Live CD

To install Linux from a live CD, you will first need to download the appropriate file. Before you do this, you will need to select your distribution and visit the homepage. From there, you can go through the downloads page and find the file that is suited to your system. There are usually a few different files for each system: some are optimized for netbooks and others for desktops, offering both 32- and 64-bit versions. After you locate the version required by your system, download the .ISO file.

Once you have the file on your computer, burn it onto a blank CD. There are programs you can download for this but generally your operating system should have some built-in programs to make this step relatively simple.

After the file is burned to the CD, restart your computer. Before the operating system boots up, you will be presented with the option to enter the boot menu. In this menu, tell the computer to boot from the CD, save your options, and restart once again. If you are unsure of where to go to select these options, consult your operating system manual and look for the boot options. This should present you with a step-by-step procedure for setting the boot options.

You are then presented with the option to either install Linux or give it a try. It is highly recommended that you go through a trial run before installing Linux to ensure that you have a good feel for the desktop and that it is what you had in mind. Once you have finished your practice run, it is easy to select the option to install.

Installing from a Live USB

If you are deciding to install from a USB, which is the more contemporary option, you will need to install an extra piece of software. Unetbootin is one option if you are running Windows. It is simple to download and get the program started. From there you can decide on your distribution from the list offered and download it to your USB. Not all the distributions are offered by Unetbootin, but that doesn't limit your options. You can simply install the .ISO file from the download page of your distribution to your desktop and then have Unetbootin pick up on the file.

You then need to follow the same process as with the CD: restart your computer with the installed distribution on your drive connected and go into the BIOS, select the boot options and choose the USB hard drive as the first option on the list, save your options, and restart once again. You will be taken to the Unetbootin menu where you can start your Linux session just as you could with the live CD method.

The Installation Process

The way a distribution is installed on your system varies, but you are generally given a setup guide that walks you through the process. If you are deciding to install Linux alongside another operating system, such as Windows, there is a little bit of work that needs to be done during the installation process to ensure that everything runs smoothly.

The first step, in this case, is to partition your drive. This will tell your computer where you want Linux to be installed. This is a simple task that requires little effort on your part. You just need to select a space on your hard drive and allocate some of the free space you have for the installation and running of the operating system.

If you are installing Ubuntu, the program will generally do this for you by selecting its own space. From there, the rest of the installation process is quite simple.

For other distributions, you will be required to partition the space yourself and some partitioning tools can be pretty complex. In this case, you will need to create two new partitions. One is to set aside space for the operating system itself. The recommendation is at least 10 GB for this. You should name this partition "Ext4" and set the mount point as "/". Then create a second partition for what is called "swap space." This is where the memory well be held in order to run the operating system and keep things processing quickly. If you only have a small amount of RAM available, make the swap partition twice as large as your available memory. If you have a decent amount of RAM (over 3GB), make the swap partition the same size as your available RAM.

GRUB and other Bootloaders

Before Linux completes the installation process, it will install a new bootloader onto your system under the name GRUB. This will be replacing your standard bootloader and will give you the option upon start-up to open your desktop with Windows or Linux. You do not need to do any work during this part of the installation process; you only need to sit back and let your distribution install GRUB.

For those of you who have a Mac, this is one of the parts of the process that will work differently and you will need to install GRUB onto the Linux partition manually.

Windows users: make a note that if you decide to uninstall and reinstall Windows at any point, you will need to install GRUB manually once you get your operating system set up again.

If you prefer something with a more enhanced user interface, you may want to install another bootloader that is compatible with Linux. An example of this is a bootloader called Burg. However, you do not need to do this straight away and can wait until you have finished installing Linux before setting up a new bootloader.

If you have followed these steps, you are ready to go. Your Linux partition should now be installed and all you need to do is restart your computer to be taken to the GRUB menu. From there you can decide whether you would like to boot Linux or Windows. Obviously, for the purposes of this book, we want to boot Linux to get a feel for it for the first time. You will notice that there are several pre-installed apps that come with your Linux distribution. Some of these will be useful to you and some will not, but you can take a look at each one and figure out which ones you can use.

In some cases, installing a new operating system can cause hardware to become unstable. This is usually because the hardware does not realize that you are using Linux and some miscommunication can occur. This is especially the case for Wi-Fi. There are some steps you can take to ensure that all your hardware is compatible with your new installation. We will discuss this in the next chapter.

Chapter 3: Fine-Tuning Your Hardware

While this may not happen every time, in some cases when you install Ubuntu or some of the other Linux distributions, you will notice that not everything is working smoothly. For this chapter, we will be using Ubuntu as our example and walking through the steps to ensure that your hardware will work with your newly installed operating system.

Wi-Fi

Perhaps the most crucial of the hardware issues you will encounter is that your Wi-Fi might start acting up. The problem with having Wi-Fi issues is that you will have to grab another device to search online for a solution, but fortunately, reading through this chapter can ensure you already know how to get your Wi-Fi back up and running in the event of an issue.

You can check the compatibility of your Wi-Fi card and distribution with the Ubuntu Community documentation section where you can find people discussing their cards and any issues that they may be coming across when installing Ubuntu. You can also search for the answers to your problem and find results from other places on the internet.

If you are unable to solve your issues, there are some tools you can use to adapt your wireless card Windows driver to communicate effectively with Linux. To do this, you will need to install the Windows driver for the card to your system and then install the ndisgtk package that comes with Ubuntu. If you don't have access to internet, you can either use an ethernet cable or download the package onto a USB and connect this to your system. Then, install the package from the system and go into the Administration menu. You can then load the INF files to your Windows package using the "Install New Driver" button.

Proprietary Drivers

For those of you who don't have open source drivers, Linux is unlikely to be able to use these drivers since they do not allow users to use them for their own purposes and package them with the distributions. In this case, you will need to install new drivers manually.

There are open source drivers available for some of the more mainstream hardware drivers, such as Nouveau, which is an open source Nvidia driver and is packaged along with many Linux distributions. There is plenty of support that comes with these drivers, although they are never quite as streamlined as the proprietary drivers, which means you will need to search to find the version that will work for your distribution.

This process is different for each distribution, but in the case of Ubuntu, you have a simple and straightforward driver manager which can be found under System > Administration > Hardware Drivers. This will give you the details of all drivers available for your system, allowing you to install them with just the push of a button. Not all distributions are this simple; some require far more work through online searching or reading the documentation for the specific distribution.

You will need to go through this process for any piece of hardware that might be experiencing issues once you have installed your new operating system. These issues are nothing to be concerned about; it is just a matter of having the right software to replace the Windows drivers previously on your system.

DVDs, MP3s, Video Formats, And More

Here is where things can get a little tricky when switching over to Linux because unfortunately, there are still a lot of things missing when it comes to some distributions (such as Ubuntu), like built-in access to MP3s, DVDs, licensed fonts, and a few other items that you might not even think of when it comes to using your Windows computer. The reason for this is that licensing can be a bit confusing when it comes to open source programs, but there is a very simple way around this.

There are two steps you will need to take to install the correct items to have those features up and running:

1. If you are currently running Ubuntu, you simply need to follow this link, which will take you to the right page to start installing: www.apt:ubuntu-restricted-extras?section=universe?section=multiverse. You also have the option of using an installer from Ninite or even of going through the Ubuntu software center which can be found in your applications menu. From there you simply need to search for "ubuntu restricted," which will generate the link required for you to install the extras.

2. Once this is done, you will need to open a terminal. This can be done by going to the applications menu, clicking on accessories, and then clicking on terminal. From there you only need to enter "sudo /usr/share/doc/libdvdread4/install-css.sh".

   This should give you the supporting files you need for MP3s, commercial DVDs and most of the other video and audio formats you use on an everyday basis. You will also have support for Java and Windows-specific fonts. While Linux may present some challenges when it comes to finding the right files, the solutions are never too complex and you only need to do it when you are first installing the new operating system.

Not all distributions will lack the necessary files, some will offer their own built-in packages of restricted goods or packages available through apps. You can search through the installer package to see if you will need to find these yourself by using search terms such as "mp3" or "Windows media."

Mouse And Keyboard

For those of you who have a more advanced mouse or keyboard with extra buttons or features, such as those that are customized for gaming, you might find that you are missing some of those features after installing Linux. This can easily be fixed by letting Linux know what the purposes of all these extra buttons are. There are a few ways to remap the extra buttons on your mouse, each requiring some manual work.

The easiest way to command Linux to utilize the full potential of your mouse is by using the command 'xbindkeys'.

If you are unfamiliar with using commands, don't worry too much as it is really quite simple. As an example, we are going to take a thumb button for a mouse and remap it to "Ctrl+T," which you may know is the standard keyboard command for opening new tabs in Firefox.

The first thing we need to consider is the name of each of the buttons on our mouse to make sure we give the right command to the right button. It is difficult to do this by sight alone, so we will need to run another command to identify our available buttons: 'xev'.

You will see a small white window containing a box. Place your cursor within the white window, avoiding the box, and press the button that you would like to issue a command with. By pressing the thumb button, for example, we are given some coding which indicates the name of the button:

> ButtonPress event, serial 33, synthetic NO, window 0x4e00001,
> root 0x142, subw 0x0, time 568329, (93,19),
> root:(96,714),
> state 0x0, button 10, same_screen YES

As you can see along the bottom line, the button we just clicked is known as button 10. All we need to do now is close xev by using Ctrl+C and continue with the remapping of our keys. We then install two new programs: xbindkeys and xautomation, by running the following command.

sudo apt-get install xbindkeys xautomation

Then we create a config file for xbindkeys by running the command:

xbindkeys --defaults > /home/your-user-name/.xbindkeysrc

You will need to replace "your-user-name" with your actual username. This will provide you with a file that you can edit by opening your file browser and making sure you have hidden files shown. Once you do this, you can see .xbindkeysrc at the top of the list. By double clicking it, you will be able to enter the next line of command at the end of the file.

```
# Thumb Button = Ctrl+T
"xte 'keydown Control_L' 'key T' 'keyup Control_L'"
  B:10
```

This simulates a keypress; you want to make sure you are pressing the control key and T at the same time before releasing the control key. The B:10 at the end indicates that this command is tied to button 10 on our mouse. As you can see, this is really quite simple and can be done by just about anyone. The process can be replicated for any button that needs to be changed.

Chapter 4: Linux's Available Features

The advantages of Linux are found within the kernel. As mentioned earlier in this book, the kernel is a piece of code which is consistent throughout Linux. By understanding the Linux kernel, you can modify the operating system to include support for the features you want. Many people have altered the kernel specifically for their needs in the past, and these features have become an integral part of many Linux distributions.

Multiuser

While you can have multiple users with Windows, you lack the ability to have those multiple users logged on at the same time. This means you are limited in how many people can be working on the system at once. With Linux, multiple users can work on the system at the same time, and each user can customize their working environment to suit their own needs.

Each user has their own unique directory where files are stored, desktop with icons, menus, and applications. You are, of course, able to password protect these accounts in order to protect your applications and data, and control who is able to access them, even on the same system.

Multitasking

Linux has the advantage of being able to operate many programs at the same time. This means users are able to have programs running in the background as well as having multiple programs being run at a single time. This also allows your system to have processes running that make it possible for Linux to host a server; these system processes run in the background and communicate with the network as requests come through to log into the system, search the web, copy a file, or print a document. These processes are known as daemons.

Graphical User Interface (X Window System)

Linux offers users a powerful framework when working with anything involving graphics. This framework is known as the X Window System, also referred to as just 'X'. The X Window System manages the functions which are involved in any X-based graphical user interface applications and allows them to be displayed on those processes that are managing the devices of your computer through the server such as the screen, mouse, and keyboard.

You also have the advantage of having an X-based desktop environment which allows you to have a simulation of the desktop and window manager of your GUI complete with all the icons, window frames, menus, and colors; all the things we refer to as themes.

You have a number of options when it comes to desktop environments and managers, each with their own focus.

Hardware Support

There are a number of support options available for the hardware connected to computer. This involves anything from floppy disk drives (if you still have them), CDs, DVDs, USBs, sound cards, external tape devices, and basically anything else that is compatible with a computer system.

As we explored in an earlier chapter, it can be difficult to find the right drivers from common hardware manufacturers due to the open source nature of the operating system. However, the Linux community will often write a driver to be compatible with your distribution within a short amount of time.

Application Support

Due to the fact that Linux is compatible with POSIX, as well as a number of other application programming interfaces (or APIs), there is an immense variety of freeware and shareware software available for Linux. While it may take some streamlining and adjusting, you will be able to run most of the GNU software offered by the Free Software Foundation.

Earlier in our introduction to Linux, we discussed that Linux is an open source program with a community of users adopting and adapting the operating system to suit their needs. For this reason, the features of Linux are virtually limitless in their functionality. If you need Linux to perform a specific function, you can alter the software and even create your own distribution. While not everyone has this kind of skill, it is possible, and even likely, that the feature you are looking for is available for download.

No Spyware

Spyware has become a massive problem for many Windows users. As soon as a program is downloaded that includes spyware, it begins working. The user may be completely unaware that there are applications running in the background that are collecting user information and sending it back to third parties who use this data to potentially steal their identities or sell the information to marketing companies. These applications can also change the way the computer interprets information. As mentioned earlier, many of the viruses which are created for PCs are specific to Windows, so Linux is free from many of the most damaging viruses. Even better, there is no need to spend money on purchasing and upgrading anti-virus software or paying for costly system recovery.

No Defragmentation

Linux has a very advanced and efficient filing system which does not require the data to be defragmented. In the case of regular Windows computers, these file systems can become fragmented which can cause crashes, slowdowns, and memory loss on your system.

No Crashes

If you have a Windows computer, you are no stranger to random crashes for which you are never given a reason. For example, if you were running Windows and your browser crashed, the entire operating system could come crashing down due to the fact that the system is connected to the Graphic User Interface. This has happened to virtually every Windows user and can be incredibly frustrating when it comes to losing data or interrupting an important task. You will experience none of these crashes with Linux because the Linux core operating system (the kernel) is separated from the Graphic User Interface in the X Window, and from the applications that you use such as OpenOffice.org. If an application were to crash for whatever reason, such as a corrupted file, the core operating system would remain operational.

No Frequent Re-Installation

You will notice that one of the ideal solutions for issues with Windows is to simply reinstall the entire operating system and start from scratch. This can be difficult when it comes to the times that Windows crashes and there is no way to recover the data you have lost. If you run a business using your system, this can be incredibly costly and damaging to your business operations. Linux, on the other hand, will not crash in the same way, meaning your data is safe and recoverable if you are faced with any issues, which are, when it comes to Linux, few and far between. You are actually able to store your data separately from the operating system so that any personal user preferences are able to be stored even if you do choose to reinstall the operating system. This can be done by creating a new partition which will keep your home directory. Similarly, through Windows, you are constantly required to restart the system if any changes are made, such as installing new hardware or software, in order to reconfigure the system. In the case of Linux, there is no need for this.

Many Filing Systems

Windows comes with two filing systems. Linux, on the other hand, brings with it hundreds of filing systems, which is useful for those users who are required to work across multiple computers, exchanging hardware from one system to another.

Powerful Command Line

We have explored some of the basics of using the command line, or the shell environment. With Windows, there is not much farther you can go with the command line, especially for basic users. Linux, on the other hand, has an incredibly powerful command line, as we mentioned earlier. With Linux's command line, you can write entire programs for Linux, which means that you can eliminate repetitive tasks through automation. An example of this would be backing up your system. This is usually an extremely arduous task; imagine if you could just run a simple program that runs through the entire process with just one click. This and numerous other simplifications are all possible with the Linux command line.

Vendor Independence

With Windows, you are locked into a single vendor if you want to keep your system up-to-date. This can a disincentive for many people who don't want to keep spending money to keep their system safe. With Linux, you are never locked into a single vendor because the community offers a large variety of vendors who each have their own distributions to offer and to provide support for. If you feel that a particular vendor has let you down when it comes to support or if you have encountered a distribution that didn't live up to your expectations, you can either turn to the community for further support or adopt a new vendor altogether. You don't have to start over from scratch or feel trapped with a vendor that doesn't seem to have your best interests in mind. Even better, if a vendor happens to walk away from their distribution, you are not forced to choose a new vendor or distribution, but can instead turn to the ever-growing community to continue publishing your distribution. Keep in mind there are no licensing agreements involved when it comes to Linux, meaning you are free to download, modify, and repackage as you wish.

No Registry

If you have used registry on Windows, you will know that it can be a nightmare. Not only do you need specific tools to open and modify the files, if any of the data is corrupted, it can be extremely frustrating to manage. With Linux, most of the configuration is stored in plain text files. This allows you to easily manage, backup, and transfer these files between systems. This is much simpler than using registry.

High Degree of Documentation

Have you ever had an issue that you simply could not find a solution for? You look through the manual only to come up empty-handed, you search through forums and search engines looking for an answer, but there is just no record of anyone else having the same issue. This is hardly ever the case for problems with Linux. Linux is one of the most documented operating systems and almost all of these documents are free of charge. The documents are not PDFs thrown together by just anyone, but are well-written documents which detail many of the concepts that help explain the inner-working of Linux. This is perhaps one of the greatest advantages to the Linux community, which is comprised of a number of online forums, articles, and groups that are located in virtually every country, city, and town. This means that you are never very far from another Linux user in the case that you would like to have someone help you out with the systems workings in person.

You will find that the community almost behaves like a family since everyone has the same goals and objectives when it comes to improving and developing the open source operating system.

The best Linux experience is unlocked when you get involved in this community and offer value to other members, who will surely return the favor.

Package Management

The excellent package management offered by Linux allows users to access tools which can simplify the process of installing and upgrading applications. In addition to this, if you were to upgrade your current distribution of Linux, this is really quite simple. Furthermore, if you are a developer, you have access to a wide range of development tools, libraries, and compilers which come along with the package. For those who are Java developers or Web developers who use PHP/Perl/Ruby or C and C++ coding, you can put your skills to good when using Linux. This gives developers the freedom to use Linux as they wish and even offer and share their own versions of Linux with the community, their friends, and their family.

No Open Ports

One major issue with Windows computers is the fact that unused ports are left open. This can lead to attacks by hackers that can disable and take control of your computer to either inflict harm on your system or carry out further attacks using your computer as a kind of attack zombie. Linux leaves no open ports, which means your data is highly secure and protected from unauthorized entry.

Faster Release Cycle

The patches that are created for Linux distributions are written within hours rather than days or weeks in the case of other operating systems. This means if there is a known issue or threat to the security of your system, patches, which offer protection, will be created much faster than in the case of proprietary software. Additionally, many of the Linux distributions are set to be released every 6 months, making it easy to gain access to the latest application updates, patches, and bug fixes, as well as improvement and support for newer hardware that you have integrated into your system. Windows, on the other hand, has an inconsistent release cycle. Sometimes it can take years for a reliable release with some of the releases being poor and full of bugs, really not even worth upgrading to.

Total Control

Using Windows can sometimes feel as though you are on a runaway train. You have applications and processes opening that you have very little understanding of. Sometimes you many not even know what a program is, or what it is doing to your computer. This can be not only confusing, but it can also take up precious memory which should be allocated to the programs you want and need. With Linux, you have greater control over what applications are running and updating, as well as when they do so. You will need to give permission before a program opens so you always know exactly what is occurring on your computer.

You also have full control over the GUI that is operating on your system. If you wanted to change the type of GUI you are using with Windows, you would be unable to do so as you only have one default GUI. Linux offers an extensive variety of GUIs, which are (ironically) called Window Managers. You can select a GUI that you feel works best for the way you use your system. There are dozens of options, from beautiful graphic-heavy GUIs to fast, streamlined options. There are also options that are great for beginners, a few of which, like Gnome and KDE, have been mentioned in earlier chapters.

Bundles

Windows generally avoids bundling applications with the operating system other than a simple text editor, an image-editing application, and a few others. Many of the applications that are worthwhile require external downloading and installation and often come with a high price tag. Linux bundles many different applications with the distributions. These range from some of the more well-known programs like the Office Suite and photo-editing software, to some open source applications that might be new to you. The advantage is that these applications will come with your distribution free of charge. They improve your computer experience with no extra fees involved. Some of these open source programs are available to download and use on a Windows system, but this takes download and installation time, whereas with Linux they are already available by default. These bundles can be massive, with thousands of applications, some boasting over 20,000 of them.

For those applications that you do need to download onto your system, you can do this through the included app store. With Ubuntu, the built-in app store has thousands of applications which can be easily downloaded with a single click.

Browsing Benefits

Most Linux distributions come bundled with Mozilla Firefox, which most of you will be familiar with. Firefox is a powerful browser with a number of built-in features, such as ad-blocking, pop-up restriction, and a number of other advantages over the standard browser packaged with Windows. Linux also makes browsing simpler and faster due to Linux's improved networking capabilities that save bandwidth and ensure a stable internet connection.

No Automatic Updates

Automatic updates are often touted as a benefit of Windows, but this process can be not only annoying, but also harmful to the ways in which you are using your system. Most people probably have no idea what files are actually being updated. With Linux, you have the option to click and apply the update rather than this happening without your consent. You are welcome to set up your own automatic updates if you wish, but you do not have to just accept them. With Linux, you are given total control over when, how, and what your computer will be updating.

3-D Desktop

Linux allows users to take advantage of an advanced 3-D desktop with Compiz, allowing you to switch and view multiple desktops simultaneously. This feature was considered quite advanced when it was created, miles ahead of Windows. Even now, Compiz is one of the most streamlined 3-D desktops and takes up little memory on the graphics cards.

Chapter 5: Using The Linux Command Line

We have already covered what the command line is and a few of the basics, but now it is time to jump in a little deeper and see what is really possible. In this chapter, we will be exploring some of the functions of the command line interface and its advantages over the graphical user interface. While the GUI is great for beginners and users who have just installed Linux to get a feel for their new operating system, the true power is found within the command line. This is where we are truly able to make Linux work for us.

The command line allows you to work outside the limitations of your distribution. Relying on your distribution means you will become accustomed to performing tasks a certain way, and if you then need to change distributions for some reason, you will have to relearn even some of the most basic tasks because there are many different ways to perform tasks across distributions. Depending on the distributions you are moving between, this can be quite a complex undertaking and using the command line enables you to skip this adjustment and stay in control regardless of the distribution you are using.

By understanding the Debian-based systems, you are able to use basic commands such as "apt-get" or "dpkg" to manage your software, regardless of the distribution you are using. This also allows you to avoid the pain of discovering that the distribution you are using is missing some of the features you have become accustomed to, or of discovering that these features were hidden in the updated GUI.

There are more advantages to using the command line than just having control over the features available to you. Using a GUI can cause many of the system's resources to be consumed, slowing down your system and causing tasks to take much longer than they would take if you were using the command line.

The command line can be quite intimidating at first, but once you understand the language, it is as simple as sending a message to your PC with some instructions on what you need it to do. Imagine texting a teenager for the first time and not understanding the lingo. Similarly, not knowing the command line language can make you feel pretty out of the loop and confused. Once you know it though, you can communicate with ease and hopefully avoid embarrassing yourself.

Getting The Shell

Before you are able to start typing commands to your computer, you will need to run the shell. The shell is the program which creates the orders for the computer using the text that you input. There is a specific set structure of commands which will be unique to your OS, as different operating systems use different structures when performing similar tasks.

For this reason, there are many different shells available for Linux, but the most common and popular one, which is recommended since it will have the largest community support, is BASH (Bourne-Again shell). BASH was written by the GNU Project and is the best go-to for beginners. There are other options if you prefer something more modern with a few extra features such as "zsh," which can easily be installed from your distribution.

If you are working from a desktop environment, then it is best to use a terminal emulator in order to emulate the terminal for that particular interface. You will find that different distributions will come with their own specific terminal emulators. For example, KDE comes with Konsole, and Gnome uses Gnome Terminal.

Your First Commands

When opening the terminal emulator, you will notice that you are in the home directory of the logged-in user by default. This can be seen with the name of the logged-in user prior to the hostname. Seeing the $ symbol indicates that you are logged in as a regular user, while seeing the # symbol indicates that you are logged in as a root.

It is best to avoid working on the command line as a root as this can change the permissions of all the files you have been working on as well as their directions, and make the root the user of the directions and files within. If you are performing administrative tasks, however, or working inside root directory, then there is no issue being logged in as a root user.

If you would like to see all the directions and files that are in the current directory you are working in, you can do this by listing them all with the "ls" command which is the following line of command:

> [swapnil@swaparch ~]$ ls

> Desktop Documents Downloads Music Pictures Public Templates Videos

Changing Locations

You can move about through your system by first changing to any directory through the use of the "cd" command. If you feel like taking a shortcut, you are also able to use the tab key to automatically complete the path. To enter directories, you simply need to use forward slash. For example, if you would like to go into the downloads directory inside the home folder, you use cd to command a change in directory, followed by the path you would like to travel. You will need to use your username as part of the command. For this example, we will use "swapnil":

> Documents/ Downloads/

> [swapnil@swaparch ~]$ cd /home/swapnil/Downloads/

> [swapnil@swaparch Downloads]$

You will notice in the third line, we have our directory, "Downloads," located inside some square brackets. This indicates that the move has been successful and we are now located inside the directory. If you would like, you can see the subdirectory and files located inside Downloads by using the "ls" command once again.

Keep in mind that you don't need to provide the complete path when moving around inside a subdirectory if you are coming from the current directory. For example, if you would like to travel to a subdirectory known as "Test," which is located within the downloads directory, all you need to do is type "cd" and then the directory name, which would be written as "Test," without requiring the forward slash.

[swapnil@swaparch Downloads]$ cd Test

When changing from one directory to another, you simply need to follow that same procedure by using "cd PATH_OF_DIRECTORY." In order to reverse your steps and go back to the directory that you just came from, you will need to use "cd ../" and if you need to go back even further, say two directories, you would the use "cd ../../," The more directories you are retracing, the more you extend the command line in that way.

If you would like to have a peek at the content located within a directory, you don't need to change directories. Instead you can use the "ls" command, but in a slightly different way:

ls /PATH_OF_DIRECTORY

Going back to our previous example, if we wanted to look in the Test folder without having to go there we simply type in:

[swapnil@swaparch ~]$ ls /home/swapnil/Downloads/Test/

In the case that a directory is hidden, you are still able to see it by using a special option within the "ls" command. Following "ls," you simply need type in "-a," as in the example below:

[swapnil@swaparch ~]$ ls -a /home/swapnil/Downloads/Test/

Determining Size

What if you need look at the size of the directories you are working in? Is this possible with the command line? Yes! And it's really quite simple. You will only need to use the "-l" option along with the "ls" command. This will also give you a breakdown of some other information, such as the permissions of the files and directories, who their owners are, as well as the time and date of the latest modification.

```
[swapnil@swaparch ~]$ ls -l
/home/swapnil/Downloads/Test/

total 4

drwxr-xr-x 2 swapnil users 4096 Mar 26 11:55 Test_2
```

As you can see, the command provides the file size in a way that can be a little difficult to make sense of. There is a way we can change this format to have it presented in a way that makes it more understandable and readable for those who might not be familiar with the coding. All we need to do here is use the "ls -lh" command like so:

```
[swapnil@swaparch ~]$ ls -lh
/home/swapnil/Downloads/Test/

total 4.0K

drwxr-xr-x 2 swapnil users 4.0K Mar 26 11:55 Test_2
```

If you would like a breakdown of all the directories and files located within a particular location, you are able to obtain a simple list which is free of all the extra information. This can be done using the "ls -R" command. You will find that the output generated from this command can be quite long as it carries all the files located within a direction and where they are located.

Creating New Directories

Now we are able to create new directories using the command line. In order to do this, you will need to familiarize yourself with the command "mkdir." Upon entering this command, you will find that the new directory is created within the current directory by default. If you want to create this directory in another location, you can do this by providing a complete path to the location in which you desire your new directory be created:

mkdir /path-of-the-parent-directory/name-of-the-new-directory

As an example, if we wanted to create a new directory called "distros" to keep all the files that are created when we download a new Linux distribution in the downloads directory, then we would simply run the following command:

[swapnil@swaparch ~]$ mkdir /home/swapnil/Downloads/distros

Now, if we would like to create a further subdirectory inside this newly created directory, we would need to use the "-p" option in conjunction with the "mkdir" command. If you wanted to create a new directory called "distros," but also add a further directory called "opensuse" within it, you would need to let the system know that while this directory doesn't exist, you would like to create it now in order to store this new directory within it. Let's have a look at an example:

mkdir -p /home/swapnil/Downloads/distros/opensuse

What this will do is create a new directory called "distros," as well as another directory within it called "opensuse"—all with a single command. Can you do that with a fancy GUI? Not likely.

Deleting Directories

Deleting directories is just as simple and straightforward as creating them. You will need to use the command "rm" if you want to delete files, and the command "rm -r" if you want to delete a directory. Remember the difference and be aware of which command you use as it can be devastating to use the wrong one when you intend to delete files and actually end up deleting the entire directory.

> rm /path-of-the-directory-or-file

For our example, we are going to delete the opensuse directory we just created. In order to do this, we would use the command line:

> rm -r /home/swapnil/Downloads/distros/opensuse/

If we decided we would like to delete all the content within a directory but keep the directory itself, we would use the asterisk following a slash. For example, if we were to delete everything within the opensuse directory, we would use the command line:

> rm /home/swapnil/Downloads/distros/opensuse/*

In the case that there are subdirectories located inside, you would need to use the "-r" option once again in order to tell the system that you are including the sub-directories in your purge. This would appear as:

> rm -r /home/swapnil/Downloads/distros/opensuse/*

System Information

Aside from interacting with the files and directories on your system, you are also able to use the command line to gain information on the system itself. For example, if you wish to assess how much disk space is on your file system based on the partitions, you are able to use the command "df," or if you would like to read it in a more understandable way, use the command "ds -h," which will then display the report in megabytes and gigabytes. If you would like to look at the amount of free space in comparison to the used memory, use the "free" command in conjunction with "-m," which will report back the figure in megabytes.

If you would like details on the system such as the processes running and the resources available, which is useful when first adopting the command line, you can use the "top" command. This will give you a report on the running processes, the usage of your CPU and RAM, and a total number of the tasks being run, which you might like to compare with the GUI report of the same nature.

Summary

As you can see, using the command line is both simple and powerful. Rather than just relying on the GUI, which can take up valuable processing resources, the command line allows you to execute functions with precision and speed. It might seem a little daunting at first, but once you get used to it, you will find that it is a much more flexible way of interacting with your computer and with the Linux operating system. Once you become comfortable with the more basic functions of the command line, you can then move forward with advanced commands.

Chapter 6: Advanced Commands

We explored some of the more basic commands in the last chapter, such as how to navigate through directories and modify files. In this chapter, we are going to consider some more advanced commands for users who have grown accustomed to the shell and the basic commands. Keep in mind that while these are more advanced commands, they barely scratch the surface on what is possible when writing scripts in the command line. For now, let's take a look at the next level for those learning Linux commands.

Find

The find command allows you to search for particular files within a directory. This is similar to the way you would do this in your file manager, but this find command is a little more flexible and powerful in the way it tracks down your files. The find command will look through the parent directories as well as sub directory, taking note of all the files that match the options you provided. Here is an example of how this would look:

```
root@user:~# find -name *.sh
./Desktop/load.sh
./Desktop/test.sh
./Desktop/shutdown.sh
./Binary/firefox/run-mozilla.sh
./Downloads/kdewebdev-
3.5.8/quanta/scripts/externalpreview.sh
./Downloads/kdewebdev-3.5.8/admin/doxygen.sh
./Downloads/kdewebdev-3.5.8/admin/cvs.sh
./Downloads/kdewebdev-3.5.8/admin/ltmain.sh
./Downloads/wheezy-nv-install.sh
```

You will notice that we use the option "-name." This makes the option case sensitive, meaning the results will yield only those results that are similar to the case of the search term; in this case, ".sh." If you would like to search for a term regardless of the case, you simply need to use the "-iname" option. The * is a wildcard that will search all files that have the extension ".sh." You can modify this with the file name you require if you would like to get more specific results.

Command: grep

The grep command is for when you are searching a particular file in order to find a match for search terms. This is similar to the way you would search for terms in a word processing application or through your browser, but with the command line, you don't even need to open the file to search through it.

For example, if you were to look through a file, in this case "/etc/passwd" for the term "user," it would look something like this:

```
root@user:~# grep user /etc/passwd
user:x:1000:1000:User,:/home/user:/bin/bash
```

You can ignore any specific word case and other combinations by using the "-i" option, in which case the line of command would look like this:

```
root@user:~# grep -i USER /etc/passwd
user:x:1000:1000:user,,,:/home/user:/bin/bash
```

We are also able to search the entirety of the directory by using "-r." For example, if we wanted to find the string "127.0.0.1":

```
root@user:~# grep -r "127.0.0.1" /etc/
/etc/vlc/lua/http/.hosts:127.0.0.1
/etc/speech-
dispatcher/modules/ivona.conf:#IvonaServerHost
"127.0.0.1"
/etc/mysql/my.cnf:bind-address          = 127.0.0.1
/etc/apache2/mods-available/status.conf:    Allow from
127.0.0.1 ::1
/etc/apache2/mods-available/ldap.conf:    Allow from
127.0.0.1 ::1
```

/etc/apache2/mods-available/info.conf: Allow from
127.0.0.1 ::1
/etc/apache2/mods-
available/proxy_balancer.conf:#   Allow from 127.0.0.1
::1
/etc/security/access.conf:#+ : root : 127.0.0.1
/etc/dhcp/dhclient.conf:#prepend domain-name-servers
127.0.0.1;
/etc/dhcp/dhclient.conf:# option domain-name-servers
127.0.0.1;
/etc/init/network-interface.conf: ifconfig lo 127.0.0.1 up
|| true
/etc/java-6-openjdk/net.properties:# localhost &
127.0.0.1).
/etc/java-6-openjdk/net.properties:#
http.nonProxyHosts=localhost|127.0.0.1
/etc/java-6-openjdk/net.properties:# localhost &
127.0.0.1).
/etc/java-6-openjdk/net.properties:#
ftp.nonProxyHosts=localhost|127.0.0.1
/etc/hosts:127.0.0.1 localhost

There are a few options available to you when using the grep
command, such as:

- -w for word (egrep -w 'word1|word2' /path/to/file)

- -c for count (i.e., total number of times the pattern
  matched) (grep -c 'word' /path/to/file)

- —color for colored output (grep —color server
  /etc/passwd)

Command: man

This one is useful for when you are just starting out and you
want to see some of the options available for a particular
command. The man is the system's manual pager and basically

gathers all the available documentation from the internet for a command, and what each of these options do by providing manual pages for each of the options.

Command: ps

The "ps" means process and what this will do is give you a status of all the processes which are currently running on your system, along with a unique ID called PID. It will appear like this:

```
root@user:~# ps
PID TTY        TIME CMD
4170 pts/1   00:00:00 bash
9628 pts/1   00:00:00 ps
```

If you would like to see the status of the processes which are running along with their ID and PID, use the option "-A" which will appear in your command line like so:

```
root@user:~# ps -A
PID TTY         TIME CMD
1 ?        00:00:01 init
2 ?        00:00:00 kthreadd
3 ?        00:00:01 ksoftirqd/0
5 ?        00:00:00 kworker/0:0H
7 ?        00:00:00 kworker/u:0H
8 ?        00:00:00 migration/0
9 ?        00:00:00 rcu_bh
....
```

This helps you understand which processes are running, how long they have been running, and whether they are needed to be halted for whatever reason. You can combine this with the 'grep' command in order to find a customized output:

```
root@user:~# ps -A | grep -i ssh
1500 ?      00:09:58 sshd
4317 ?      00:00:00 sshd
```

Command: kill

For those processes which cease responding or are simply not relevant to your current tasks, you are able to halt them by using the kill command. This becomes quite useful when it comes to ending processes which are taking up massive amounts of CPU power but aren't actually helping you with your tasks. Often, these processes become a struggle to kill on operating systems such as Windows and can sometimes require you to restart your system altogether, but not with Linux.

The kill command works on any process (or ps). For example, if we were to kill the program "apache2," which has ceased to respond, we would need to first run "ps -A" in conjunction with the grep command:

```
root@user:~# ps -A | grep -i apache2
1285 ?        00:00:00 apache2
```

You will then see the apache2 process along with its PID, which you will use with the kill command. In this example, the process is 1285 giving way to our next command:

```
root@user:~# kill 1285 (to kill the process apache2)
```

As you can see, every time a process is run, it will generate a new PID, which you are able to identify by using the ps command.

Command: whereis

When you are looking to locate binary, source, or manual pages for a particular command, you can use the whereis command in order to reveal it. For example, if we wanted to locate the binary, source, and manual pages for the command "ls" and kill it, it would look like this:

```
root@user:~# whereis ls
ls: /bin/ls /usr/share/man/man1/ls.1.gz
```

```
root@user:~# whereis kill
kill: /bin/kill /usr/share/man/man2/kill.2.gz
/usr/share/man/man1/kill.1.gz
```

Command: service

This command allows you to control a service by either starting, stopping, or restarting the particular service. This allows you to make changes to a service without having to restart your system. The advantage of this is that you don't need to stop what you are doing to make changes to the services the computer is running.

Command: alias

This command is highly recommended for those just getting started with the shell, as it allows users to assign a name to a command that you might use often, or that is too long to enter manually every time. For example, you might be using the "ls -l" command quite frequently. The original command has 4 characters and a space, so we can use the alias command to cut this down to just one character, "l." This will help you make sense of some of those more complicated commands by using shorter terms that you are familiar with. While this is great for beginners, it is still recommended that you learn the commands before making changes, just in case you forget them in the future. Here is what it looks like in action:

```
root@user:~# alias l='ls -l'
```

You can check to see if it works by entering the command straight after like this:

```
root@user:~# l
total 36
drwxr-xr-x 3 user user 4096 May 10 11:14 Binary
drwxr-xr-x 3 user user 4096 May 21 11:21 Desktop
drwxr-xr-x 2 user user 4096 May 21 15:23 Documents
drwxr-xr-x 8 user user 4096 May 20 14:56 Downloads
```

```
drwxr-xr-x 2 user user 4096 May  7 16:58 Music
drwxr-xr-x 2 user user 4096 May 20 16:17 Pictures
drwxr-xr-x 2 user user 4096 May  7 16:58 Public
drwxr-xr-x 2 user user 4096 May  7 16:58 Templates
drwxr-xr-x 2 user user 4096 May  7 16:58 Videos
```

You can remove an alias by using the "unalias" command, which would look like this:

```
root@user:~# unalias l
```

You are then able to check if the command still exists, which it shouldn't. If you have done this correctly, you will see a message like this:

```
root@user:~# l
bash: l: command not found
```

Conclusion

Thanks again for taking the time to read this book!

You should now have a good understanding of Linux and be ready to get started with it!

If you enjoyed this book, please take the time to leave me a review on Amazon. I appreciate your honest feedback, and it really helps me to continue producing high quality books.

www.ingramcontent.com/pod-product-compliance
Lightning Source LLC
LaVergne TN
LVHW050148060326
832904LV00003B/60